Meg's tiny red teddy

Rigby®

A Harcourt Achieve Imprint

www.Rigby.com
1-800-531-5015

"Look, Mom," said Meg.

"Here is the teddy bear shop!"

3

"Here is a big teddy,"
said Mom.

"I am looking for a tiny teddy,"

said Meg.

"Here is a red teddy,"

said Mom.

"I am looking for a tiny teddy,"
said Meg.

"Here are the tiny teddies!"

said Mom.

"Here is a tiny **red** teddy,"

said Meg.

"The tiny red teddy is for you."